A Beginners Guide to Candle Making

Table of Contents

A Beginners Guide to Candle Making 1

Introduction..3

Chapter 1: Basics of Candle Making 5

Chapter 2: Different Types of Candles to Try at Home......14

Chapter 3: Special Candle Types to Try at Home 21

Chapter 4: Adding Colors, Shapes and Fragrance...............27

Chapter 5: Candle Surface Decoration Ideas.......................33

Conclusion 38

Introduction

Candles are widely used nowadays for decorative purposes considering them to be the most practical and versatile home decor. They add more tranquility to the place and create a serene ambience that is loved by all. Candle making is not just a hobby or interest, but it is an art. For ages, different designs of candles are being crafted and used for basic lighting and decorative purposes. Today, candles are used for purposes such as aromatherapy, air purification, meditation etc.

Homemade candles are much better than buying plain or clichéd candle designs available at home. If you learn the candle making skill perfectly, then it takes only few minutes to create amazing candle designs at home. Candle making can be pursued as a good home business too if you get a little creative with your skills. Many homemakers across the world supplement their household income by selling homemade candles that are personalized too.

Candle making is also the best way to distress and relax your mind. It also helps people in developing their own imagination while having fun with colors, scents and also with sparkles.

This book features the basics of candle making craft at home with proven ways to make therapeutic, eco-friendly, artistic and economical candles. Go through our candle making and designing tutorials to understand and adapt the skill set needed to create candles easily at home.

Chapter 1: Basics of Candle Making

Candle making is a skill that can be pursued to add style to your home, fill your home with a pleasant aroma and also to add more light to the interior when needed. Candle making is simple and interesting only when you learn certain knick knacks involved in it. To get started with your candle making hobby, you must first know about the candle making essentials you need at home.

The candle making supplies including the wax, molds, coloring agents, scented oils etc. are available at almost all leading supermarkets, at the grocery stores and also at art and craft stores. Nowadays there are good numbers of online hobby ideas, websites that sell candle making kits at an affordable price range.

1.1: Candle Making Essentials

Make sure you fill your arts galore or the craft box with all the below mentioned supplies needed to make candles at home.

- **Wax** – Wax is the basic raw material you need at home to make candles. There are three different varieties of wax used for making candles at home. The most common wax type is paraffin wax. Paraffin wax is available as wax chips and they are also available in the form of wax bars. Soy wax is made of soybeans and they are easy to use for candles. Soy wax is also eco-friendly, hence they can be used for sensitive candle types like votive, floating candles, etc. Beeswax is also used for candles, but they do not retain the scent or color like other types of wax meant for candles.

- **Working board** – You may need a flat working board made of plywood or any other wood with smooth surfaces to keep things flat and also to protect your floor from wax spill.

- **Heating equipment** – The heating equipment to make candle can be anything from an induction stove or a normal gas burner with a medium to low flame option.

- **Melting pan** – A melting pan with a convenient brim to pour the melted wax safely inside the candle mold is a must. The melting pan can also be a heat resistant stainless steel container with thicker bottom.

- **Stearin** – This is an additional component added to paraffin wax because the paraffin wax will become really hard once it cools down. To ease the process of removing cold candles from the mold stearin is used.

- **Wicks** – wicks are available in all stores that sell wax and other candle making essentials. Wicks are available for candles in different sizes and in different diameter. The thickness of the wick also depends on the size and the diameter of your candle.

- **Wick sustainers** – these are nothing but the equipment used to hold the candle wick in the right position as soon as you fix it in your candle mold. Also for making votive candles, these sustainers are needed to prevent the wicks from getting loose or moving sideways when the hot wax is poured inside the container.

- **Thermometer** – to make candles at home and also to check the right temperature of the wax melted in the heating container, a candy thermometer that has the range between 0-300 degree Farenheit is needed.

- **Vegetable oil spray or paper towel** – you can either use appear towel dipped in vegetable oil to seal the inside of the container so that the finished candle does not leave a thin film of residue inside the mold. The best way to prevent cold wax from the candle sticking to the container is to spray vegetable oil inside the mold before pouring hot melted wax inside it.

- **Measuring jar** – to measure the amount of wax needed to make certain types of candles, a measuring jar that manages at least 10 ounces of wax is needed.

- **Water container with water** – container filled with water is needed to sink the mold with hot wax for cooling down.

- **Scissors and tape** – to cut and tape, raw materials to get the perfect and shape for the candles.

- **Colors** – solid dyes, candle coloring chips, wax crayons and liquid candle coloring agents can be used to add colors to the candles.

1.2: Step-By-Step Candle Making Procedure

Here is a simple step-by-step procedure to effortlessly make candles at home. The basic preparation step remains the same whereas you can improvise during the decoration to make your candle look unique.

1. **Working board** – keep the working board ready so that you will do all your candle making work on it except for the heating procedure.

2. **Preparing wax**–wax should be in the form of chips or shredded to make a candle. If it is wax chips, then plainly keep it ready. In case of bar wax you must first shred the wax using a shredder and keep it ready.

3. **Wax Wick priming**–Take the candle wick and then do wax wick priming on it. Heat a little amount of wax and dip the wick in the wax. Let one end of the wick firmly tied to the wick sustainer (an iron or any other metal stick) and dip it in the hot wax. Now hold the wick in airy space for a minute till the wax cools down. Repeat this process twice to get firmer candle wicks.

4. **Preparing mold** – now take the candle mold, spray vegetable oil in the mold so that the wax after cooling down does not stick to it. Heat the mold a little by keeping it in the oven for about 30 seconds.

5. **Setting wick** – place the candle wick with sustainer on top of the mold and let the wick reach the bottom surface of the mold where there is a small hole to pull it outside. Now put a knot towards the end of the candle mold using the wick so that it does not become loose or cross.

6. **Heating wax** – heat the wax in a saucepan by keeping the heat low. Let the wax fully melt so that you can slowly add color to the wax if you need wax candle. Add scented oil to the melted hot wax after adding color if you wish to make scented candles. Stir well in mild heat so that color, wax and oils blend well.

7. **Filling or Pour** – now slowly pour the hot melted wax inside the mold while you seal the end of the mold where wick is peeping out with some dry wax.

8. **Re-**pour – let the wax cool down a little so that it forms a thin film on the top. When this happens, your candle inside the mold will look little less in the middle portion like a pothole. Now again heat the wax in the saucepan and re-pour the wax inside the mold by poking smaller holes in the centre portion of the half-set candle inside the mold. Follow the re-pour process till you find no depression towards the top of the candle as it cools down. Re-pour is actually done to fill the gap inside the setting candle that is caused by air bubbles.

9. **Final step** – as the mold cools well, you can put it inside the water container to compress the wax further. Now take out the mold from the water container and remove the mold to get your beautiful candle.

Decoration on the candle can be done after you take out the basic candle from the mold. The process remains the same for almost all types of candles.

Chapter 2: Different Types of Candles to Try at Home

There are countless designs, shapes, and in different sizes candles can be made at home. To our surprise there are even gel candles available in the market to prepare them at home, you need to be a candle making expert. However, all candle types will majorly fall under the following five top candle categories.

1. **Pillar candles**—Pillar candles are the most amazing candle type to try at home. This is the basic candle variety and easy for almost all beginners to start making the same at home. To make pillar candles you only the basic round shaped pillar candle molds that is available in different shapes, sizes, in different diameter and also in different length of the container. As mentioned in the previous chapter, you can prepare the candle wick, tie it with the wick sustainer and fill the mold with hot wax till the complete candle is well-set for hours. There are countless varieties of pillar candles you can try at home like

- **Single shade pillar candle** – just pour one shade of hot wax inside the candle mold and set it.
- **Mixed shade** – you can first mix one shade of wax, let it settle for few minutes and then heat another shade of wax, pour it inside the mold and mix using a stick to get multiple colorful candle shade.
- **Multiple layered pillar candles**–you can fill multiple layers of mold by filling in colors one by one. Ensure that you let one color settle first and then go for the next to get a perfect multiple layers of an interesting pillar candle.
- **Rustic pillar candles**–to create a rustic effect on the candle instead of creating a smooth and polished effect, you just have to cool the mold inside the chiller unit in your fridge first. The cold mold will shock the hot wax and create a rustic surface on the outer layer to create this amazing pillar candle.

Pillar candles with aroma products can also be created by adding coffee beans, potpourri, dried flowers, tea leaves, lemon peel, etc. inside your candle mold as you fill it with hot wax.

2. **Container candles** – Container candles are nothing but candles created using containers. There are different varieties of containers used to create container candles like glass containers, tin, hard plastic, metal, etc. The glass container candles are considered as the best variety of container candles because you can experiment with colors, shades and with flowers etc. in it.

All you need is a fire proof container that can sustain the heat caused when you light the candle and also handle the wax that melts inside as the candle burns. Coffee container, jam jars and jelly glass jars are the best to make glass container candles. However, there are special shapes of glass containers available in the market nowadays to make glass container candles. There are three basic styles which you can make container candles:

- **Basic container candles** – For making basic container candles you need all candle making supplies with a simple glass container. Just get the wick right and set it on the jar using the wick sustainer and finally pour the colored wax inside the container to get desired candle. Ensure you poke holes in the candle when it is half set and repeat the re-pour process many times.

- **Layered container candles** –For making layered container candles just our different colors of melted wax in different layers after one color cools off inside the container and becomes firm.

- **Marbled container candles**–To create a marbled pattern inside the container you smut first pour a basic color wax and set it for a few minutes. Let the wax settle a little so that you can poke holes inside the candle and then fill each hole with one color hot wax.

Finally, use a stick to create the marbled effect while the new colors of hot wax reach inside the container

3. **Dipped candles**– Just like the name says, dipped candles are dipped in hot wax for multiple times to get the right layer, thickness and firmness. Making dipped candle is very simple. Just prepare the candle wick and tie it straight in a spoon. Now hand the spoon in a hanger and let the candle wick reach the lower part of the hanger. Heat wax and dip the prepared wick inside the hot wax and let it cool for a few minutes and again repeat the process till you get the final product.

Dipped candles can be relatively thin, but they make the perfect candle type if you are looking for candle business. You can create dipped candles in various shades and in different layers too.

4. **Votive candles**–Votive candles are the widely used candle variety across the globe. They are simple, cute and perfect for any ambience.

Simply heat wax after preparing smaller candle wicks. Now fill the molds available for votive candles in different shapes and sizes using the hot wax. Finally, dip in the candle wick when the wax starts to cool and settle a little. Hold the wick in a straight position so that it does not go cross.

Votive candles can be made in different colors, shapes, sizes and in multiple shades too. There are paper cup votive candles, shell votive candles, rustic votive candles, ice votive candles, mosquito repellent votive candle that has tea tree oil and more can be made at home. Since the making procedure is simple for this candle variety you can focus about candle surface decoration ideas.

5. **Rolled candles** – Rolled candles are made using beeswax and they are simple to create at home. Just buy wax sheets available in the stores. Now prepare candle wick and start rolling the sheet by keeping the wick at the center. You can use a little bit of heat to stick

one wax sheet with the other and get rolled candles in different thickness and designs.

Chapter 3: Special Candle Types to Try at Home

Here are some interesting candle varieties to try at home. These candle designs are best suited for festivities, for gifting, etc. You may not find these festive or special varieties of candles easily at shops hence you can always make them at home and customize them the way you want.

1. **Balloon candles**–These candles are easy to try at home and they make the best outer shell for hurricane candles or any other votive candles. The procedure to make balloon candles is very simple. You must first fill a balloon with water and freeze it. Do not make the balloon extremely big you can just make it to twice the size of an apple. Once the balloon with water is frozen now take it out and start dipping it in hot wax by holding the other end of the balloon with a metal string. Get the thickness you need for your shell by dipping the balloon inside the hot wax. Finally, open the balloon let go of the water once the wax cools down. Scrape out the extra chunks or

edge of the balloon candle to create an opening where you will place your votive.

2. **Chunk candles** – Chunk candles are extremely easy to make but they look extremely artistic. Or gifting, if you use chunk candles, they make classy and elegant look. However, chunk candles can be made only with pillar candle molds. All you need is an extra cookie sheet prepped with vegetable oil. Melt wax in a darker shade first and then pour it on the cookie sheet. As the wax cools better, you can use a pen knife to cut it like how you cut chocolates or milk cakes. Now use these wax blocks inside the mold and fill the extra space inside the mold with a lighter shade of hot wax. Follow the pour and re-pour procedures to make the best chunk candles that look attractive too.

3. **Bloody pillar candle** – This bloody pillar candle is the best for the Halloween season and it is extremely simple to make at home. Use your pillar candle mold to make regular white

candles. You can add stearic acid to the hot wax as you melt it just to add a bright white to the candle so that bleeding looks effective. Now let the white candle cool down and settle over a day or two. To add the bleeding effect to the candle you first need to melt a wax and then add dark red color to the hot wax. Now let the wax cool a little so that it leaves a thin film and becomes thick. Just take one spoon and mix the red wax so that it gets little lumps and also appears red and thick like blood. Finally, pour the red wax on top of the white candle to get the bleeding effect.

To get the bleeding effect right on the candle you can try dipped bleeding candles too. First dip few layers of the inner portion in red color and then dip the outer layers in white color to get the bleeding effect right on your candle.

4. **Cupcake candles** – Get cupcake molds and make darker shades of votive candles in it like dark brown, light brown, red to get the red velvet cake shade, coffee, etc. once the smaller

cupcake candles are ready it is time to add whisk cream on top of them. Take lighter shades of wax like pink, mint green, yellow, white, etc. Heat the wax and let it cool a little till you get the thin filmy layer on top of the wax melting container. Now whisk the half hot wax so that it will start appearing like whisk cream. Finally, use a spoon to fill the top of the cupcake candle with whisk cream till you get the desired shape. Add smaller red candle chips on top to decorate the cupcake candles.

5. **Ice candles** – These candles are extremely artistic and they are quick to try at home. Before pouring the hot wax inside your pillar candle or votive candle mould just fill it with half crushed ice cubes. Now slowly pour the hot wax inside the mould till it reaches the brim of the mould. Let the ice cool off and you can remove the excess water from the mould first and on next day you can remove the candle from the mould. These iced candles look extremely artistic and beautiful. To make these ice candles look extra beautiful you can fill the

gaps (only few) the ice has created by adding some glitter, candle chips, by sticking candle stones etc. on them.

6. **Glitter candles** – Glitter or the sparklers can be added to the candles in two ways. One simple way is to decorate the candle by adding glue to the outer layer of the candle and then by sprinkling powder glitter on top of it. The next best way is to mix glitter with hot wax and then pouring it inside the mold. When you mix glitter with hot wax, it settles at the bottom of the mold, hence you need to stir the heating container till you pour the hot wax inside the mold.

7. **Pillar candles with faded edges**–This is simple to make at home and easy to innovate consistently. Just add white or a lighter shade of wax inside the candle mold first. Let it cool down a little bit and then add a darker shade of inner wax towards the centre portion of the candle wick. Let the candle cool inside the mold so that it looks absolutely stunning and beautiful. You can reverse the fade effect by

first adding darker shade of wax to the candle mold and then by adding lighter shade.

There are other beautiful types of candles too, that you can easily try at home by innovating the regular candle making process. Just ensure you set your wick perfectly so that you will always get your candle right. You can emboss dried flowers and leaves on your candle by heating them and then by creating patterns on the surface of the candle after you remove them from the mold.

Chapter 4: Adding Colors, Shapes and Fragrance

Colors, scent and the unique shape of the candles make them look extra special. Adding colors and scent of the candles is extremely simple, but you need to master the skill so that you remain successful every time. For both bigger and smaller candles you can add different colors, shapes and also fragrance. To start with, let's read in detail about adding scent to the candles.

Adding fragrance or scent of candles

To add unique fragrance or scent of the candles, there are exclusive candle scents available in the candle essentials store. Or you can go to any nearby fragrance selling stores and buy liquid scents. The most aromatic candles are the ones made using the local scents available in wide varieties at the scent stores. These normal scents will cost you less than $3 only. IF you wish to make classy scented candles then you can consider adding your perfume to the candles too when they are in the mold. The other best source to add aroma to your candles in an eco-friendly manner you can use aromatic oils like tea tree oil, chamomile oil, lavender oil, orange oil, etc. These oils are added to the hot wax to add a special aroma to your candles made at home.

Here is a step by step procedure to add permanent fragrance to the candles:

1. Heat the wax and let it melt fully and set the container with candle wicks.
2. How add at least 1 ounce of candle scent to the hot wax that is about 300 ml.
3. Stir the hot wax well, so that the scent or the fragrance mixes well and not only settles at the bottom of the container.
4. Now slowly pour the fragrance hot wax inside the mold and let it cool by creating the depressing op top of the candle.
5. Now use a wooden stick to poke holes on the surface of the candle and again pour the hot scented wax in the mold to set the candle.

For candle sheets and also for dipped candles too, you can add scent or fragrance by adding a melted scented candle on top of the sheet in a thin layer of wax.

Candle Coloring

To add amazing colors to your candles you can make use of the candle dyes available in the market. Candle dyes are available in exclusive colors and also in basic colors too. There are more than few hundred shades of candle dyes available. There are basically liquid candle dyes and color block candle dyes available in the market. Few people make use of food colorants to add color to their candles, but this does not give you the recommended shades or color effects, hence color block candle bye or liquid candle dye is recommended to color your candles.

Other candle colorants like crayons, candle glitters, oil pastels are also used to add colors to the candles made at home. Using colored wax crayons is the handiest and an affordable option if you wish to color the candles you make at home. There are also candle supplies stores online that sells concentrated candle coloring powders at affordable rates online.

To add color to your candle you must add the coloring agent to the hot wax while it is inside the container itself so that the color mixes well with the white candle chips to give you the perfect color or shade you need.

In case if you don't find the shades you need in the market, you can then mix two or more colors to get the desired colors. For example, pink can be added to blue to get a perfect purple shade. Mix yellow with red to give the candle an orange shade. Add pink color with yellow candle color to get a beautiful coral shade to your candle. Follow these color tricks too to get unique candle colors:

- **Layered effect** - Add one color to the bottom of the mold and then let the wax cool down for half day. Now add the next color to the mold and follow the pour and re-pour process to set the candle perfect and get the layered coloring effect.

- **Marbles effect** – use a wooden stick to mix the colors inside the candle mould after pouring in more than three colors to get the unique marble effect in your candle. In case if you wish to get the marbled effect in a white candle, then first pour in the white color candle and then let it cool for an hour. Now you can poke small holes inside the candle and fill it with newly heated color wax. Now, finally use the wooden stick to get the desired marble effect in your pure white candle.

- **Conical layers** – to add conical layers instead of round, flat layers you must first pour one color of hot wax into the mold and keep the container towards one side so that the candle sets in properly. Now add one more hot wax shade to the candle, but keep the mold in the opposite direction so that the other end of the mold has a new layer and not in plain round or flat shape. Continue doing this till you fill the mold with wax.

- **Color blocks** – add first a light color candle to the mold by melting a light color wax and then pouring it inside the mold. While you pour the hot wax, drop one by one color candle blocks and let them dissolve, but not get settled at the bottom of the mold. Finally, set the candle by letting it cool and then take out. These color block colors may not look exclusive, but once the candle is lit and starts to melt you will find the candle bleeding different colors. Use a candle stand to make these candles look extremely beautiful and unique.

Shapes – To add shapes to your candles there are different designs of candle molds available at the stores. There are round ones, flat ones, conical ones, square, rectangular, egg-shapes, heart shaped candle molds and more. You can make use of different designs of candle molds to create different shapes of candles at home.

Chapter 5: Candle Surface Decoration Ideas

There are hundreds of surface decoration ideas available to make your candles look an amazing and extremely beautiful. Surface decoration is the most artistic way to make your candle look interesting. Few simple hacks can make your candle look beautiful, but if you pay little extra attention, then the candle will look like a designer candle. Here are some useful candle surface decoration tips you can try at home for almost all types of candles you make at home.

- **Adding glitters** – to add glitter and the shimmer effect to your candles you can simply brush a layer of hot wax on the outer walls of the candle and sprinkle the glitter on the surface till you get the desired effect.

- **Polka dots** – polka dot candles look very pretty and it makes a perfect décor for almost any interior. For plain walls polka dotted candles make a perfect room interior decoration component. Just melt hot wax in a darker shade if it is a lighter candle or melt lighter wax shade if it is a darker candle shade. Remove the mother candle from the mold and ensure it is fully set. Now heat the wax for polka dots and let it cool down a little. Now use an ink filler to suck in the half cooled wax and slowly keep polka dots on the mother candle. Let the dots settle and then move the candle so that you get perfect dots.

- **Painting candles with wax** – use wax crayons to paint the fully set candles with wax. Melt wax crayons and use a brush to paint the color candles on the surface of the main candle to get the desired effect. You can also use acrylic colors or fabric colors to paint the outer sides of the candle and then coat with a thin layer of varnish to make the candle look amazing.

- **3D painting tips** – to give 3D painting effect on your candle you will first need a carving needle and a carving knife. Now carve out the outer side of the candles to get the desired shape you need and then paint the surface either with melted crayons or with fabric painting and finally coating the same with a thin layer of varnish.

- **Stencilling candle** – to stencil the candles you can use scissors to get the desired effect and then cleaning the surface with a soft tissue.

- **Applique work** – to add applique work to your candle made at home, you can make use of dry flowers, leaves, grass, herbs, etc. when the candle is fully done and taken out of the mold, simply let it fully cool. Now dip the basic applique material in the melted wax of a similar color and stick it to the candle to get the desired effect.

- **Hot knife** – use the hot knife to carve our designs on top of the candle to give some extra embossed designs and then use a hot needle with grip to give a perfect finish to the candle.

- **Beads and mirrors** – Use a little bit of hot wax a candle glue to stick the other materials to the candles. Simply line up the beads and mirrors and then use the hot wax as a glue to stick them on top of the candles to get a beautiful decoration done.

- **Candle flowers** – to do surface decoration to your candles made at home, you can use wax flower itself. Simply pour hot wax on a cookie sheet and create different flowers when the wax on the sheet is ⅓ set and flexible to fold. Now make flowers like roses, orchids, etc. using the partly hot wax sheet. Use hot wax as candle glue to stick these flowers on the sides of the candles. These flowers on the top of the candles can be colored, can be added with beads, mirrors and even with sparkles to make the candle look super rich and amazing.

You can use thread strings to create special strings on top of your candles to get the perfect thread effect. Similarly, use a hot string made of metal to create a swirl effect on the candles.

Conclusion

Candle making at home assures you fun and it is a quality hobby idea, but you have to be really careful as you deal with heat, stove, hot wax, etc. Always ensure you have a bucket full of sand near you as you melt the wax using a stove. In case if the wax melting saucepan catches fire, immediately try to extinguish it or if the situation goes out of control, use sand to extinguish fire. Similarly, you can use rags, paper and even working near water containers also help you in dealing with an emergency situation.

In case, if you have spilled or poured hot wax on your skin, then make a fine paste with baking soda and water and apply it on the burnt skin to relieve from pain and unwanted skin swelling. Use a thick glove to protect your hands as you deal with the wax. Use newspapers to cover the working area just in case if you think there will be too much spilling of wax. It is hard to clean wax settled on top of your kitchen counter, hence use paper or old cloth to cover your kitchen countertop.

After removing candles from the mold you can simply dip the mold in hot water so that unwanted residue from the mold will automatically come to the brim of the container with hot water. Follow all safety measures and enjoy making beautiful and artistic candles at home.

Made in the USA
Lexington, KY
21 May 2018